DAUGHTER OF

…a story of initiation

… a celebration of menarche.

…a reclamation of magic, mystery, and power

FOR THE YOUNG WOMAN IN US ALL

…with love

Sarah-Jayne Grace

ISBN:

978-1-9168955-0-8 - EBOOK

978-1-9168955-1-5– Paperback

DEDICATION

For Gwen and Iris may your hearts always be wild and your bodies your own…

thank you for bringing me such wisdom and reminding me how to play…

For all the young women and girls within us all…may you know the beauty, magic, and potency of this sacred time and in each cycle of life; the honour of cycling like the Great Mother – Nature herself.

And for little Sarah-Jayne …it took me an age to find you and love you…now I promise to never let you go.

CONTENTS

	Acknowledgments	i
1	Daughter of the Moon	
2	Rites of Passage Ceremony Sarah-Jayne Grace	Pg 28
3	Modern Day Ceremony Rachael Crow	Pg 34
4	The Science of Menarche	Pg 43
5	Resources	Pg 46
6	Final Notes	Pg 50
7	About the Author	Pg 51
8	Notes/Songs/Resources	Pg 53

ACKNOWLEDGMENTS

Gwen, thank you for the beautiful images and the bravery in which you stepped forward to offer illustrations for this book. I am passionate about empowering others, and it felt right to have a young woman offer images for this piece so thank you for being that person! To all those on my Creative Writing Course with New Writing South thank you for listening to my 'lyrical' banter, Lucy Colwell for the invitation to write, for tea and showing me what family is. For my Hastings Community especially Anna, Gabrielle, Sarah, and ALL those who danced with me and trusted within the Circle of Sisters, who held me in such high esteem even when I fell far short of deserving it or lost sight of myself. Viryapuspha and Paris for the friendship and aga suppers. Emma and Matt at Seakale in St Leonard's my favorite place thanks for nourishing me; food always served with love and a warm smile. To my clients over the years and those to come, thank you for having faith in the process, yourselves and allowing me to walk beside as you embarked on that journey to freedom. Thank you for being my teachers. To Gayle and Sue, gone from my life but never from my heart I thank you for leaving so I could grow, for your love may one day you forgive me. For my Shamanic Sisters and all those of the Path of Pollen, the honey and the sting always guide me. I love and am so grateful for each of you. Sally-bones I love you. Mum thanks for letting me back home! Magic, Merlin and all at Tofte for the lessons in play and love. Thank you to my new Stretch family for kicking my butt so gently but firmly! For all those out there inspiring and working with youth WE NEED YOU! Thanks, Sharon Murray, for editing and cheering me on. For Rachael for taking time to write the ceremony offered here and having faith in the story I shared so long ago. Thank you to all my teachers before and behind the veil for your wisdom and guidance and in many cases fierce compassion in keeping me focused on the fact I CAN. Mostly to acknowledge my little Sarah-Jayne who was lost for so many years in pain, now you're home I will never let you go again. YOU BELONG. YOU ARE WORTHY. I LOVE YOU.

...and for you dear reader the one who is at a stage of change may grace line your way and may you always see in the dark that you shine.

1 DAUGHTER OF THE MOON

…huddled in her favourite place, deep in the belly of her beloved oak, Bell felt safe - far away from her mother and the village as she could be. Away from the hustle and bustle, from the busybodies that wanted to know everything about her, bombarding her with questions she didn't know the answer to, asking her to talk about things she didn't want to and requesting she take part in things she didn't like. Learning how to sew or cook was not her idea of fun.

To be left with her thoughts and feelings, in silence, alone. That is what she wanted.

Here in this tree, watching the stars and moon begin their dance across the cloudless indigo sky, she could escape the strange sensations and thoughts that grew stronger each day. The pains and tugs in her belly that twisted and stabbed with a deep uncomfortable throb. Butterflies of excitement could quickly turn into moments where tears, as big as raindrops, burst forth from her eyes burning her cheeks as they fell for no reason at all.

Her growing breast buds rubbed her shirt and they felt tender and raw adding to her discomfort. Today, to avoid the feelings that pulsed through her body, she walked with hunched shoulders willing her breasts to stop developing. When they rubbed like this something so deep in her woke up. She felt she could scream aloud, just like the stray cats that wiggled their tails as they rubbed against you when you were walking in the village. Bolts of electricity (uncomfortable but strangely exciting) surged between her legs, bringing a new unfamiliar awareness to the parts of her previously ignored.

Other days she stood upright, strong, and straight, wanting to parade these mysterious growths to the world, to push them out for all to see and to feel this mix of sensations. Those days she was proud her body was finally beginning to resemble the dancing women of the village. She often watched them, shyly admiring their different shapes, each swaying with a life of its own. She'd dreamed of having parts of herself that moved like swirls and curls, resembling the snakes which slithered to their hideaway spaces in the undergrowth of the woods, captivating and magical. All different shapes and sizes. A mix of lean muscles and curves. Each their own beauty. Every woman was confident and proud.

Until now her body had never shown promise of being anything other than straight lines. Lines which helped her cut through the air when she ran to escape the feelings that grew. Chasing the birds above longing to grow wings to join them, to take flight escaping everything on the ground. Running until she could run no more.

Today was not one of those days. Today, she found herself wanting to hide, to daydream. Unable to ignore the sensations in her body, the place between her legs demanded her attention, calling for her to touch it and explore. Hesitating, she was never quite sure whether she should or not; afraid of what might happen, of what she might find, or someone else would find her and she was afraid of what they might say or do.

Sometimes she distracted herself by gazing across the water to where the bare-chested boys wrestled each other. She wished she could wrestle with them, loving the way they tested their strength, creating dust clouds as they fell in the red earth. She watched them sweat as they tussled, offering hands to one another as they slapped backs and laughed.

Other times she stole glimpses of her girlfriends giggling together. Rarely did she feel confident enough to join them. Instead, she wondered what it might be like to touch their hair and snuggle with them, how they might smell and to be held within that sound of laughter of secrets shared. Heart aching, longing to be included, yet keeping herself away, her eyes would linger for moments on their soft lips as she dreamed, distracted.

Lonely and confused, Bell longed for someone to speak to. Someone who could tell her what was happening, why she was having all these strange feelings. Someone to help her make sense of it all.

Hidden, quiet and still, comforted by the aroma of the damp moss from a tree, she sat. A short distance away she noticed a woman. She stood in the low evening tide, illuminated by the rising silvery moonlight, curvaceous and naked under a blanket of silver and white hair. It was such a strange sight, Bell wondered if she was dreaming and rubbed her eyes. Her cheeks blazed so bright, she was afraid she'd reveal herself, and so she nestled back further into her beloved oak. Rarely had she seen anyone fully naked except herself. Curious, she noticed how delicate wisps of hair raised like antennae, creating a fine halo around the woman's face as they reached towards the moonbeams above. Mesmerised, she watched as the blanket of hair swayed rhythmically, following the soft curve of her back, arms reaching out, gently moving in figures of eight, back forth, side to side in the empty space in front of her, weaving something visible only to her. Her movements mirrored the water in which she stood. Feeling herself drawn towards the woman, her body began to sway slightly in her mossy sit spot.

Through the dimming light she noticed the woman's mouth moving. On the breeze, over the short space of land and through the oak leaves, a faint thread of whispered words. They were as gentle as the softest caress reached her ears as they did if felt as though she was showered with a thousand tiny stars:

> …. *beelingeu…*

Bell's tired eyelids shuttered across her dry eyes… 'click… clack', opening and closing. Hypnotised she strained to hear. The words came again, this time clearer:

…beelingeu ta

Omna shoonla beelingeu ta tu'

The earth beneath her felt cool, a stark contrast to the soft vision before her. In the stillness she watched as a cloud of silvery mist left the woman's mouth as she spoke.

The increasingly familiar yet unfamiliar sensations again coursed through her body. Warmth, mixed with tingling, a pulse, an internal beat deep in her belly, travelling to meet at the central spot between her legs.

'Omna shoonla beelingeu ta,

Omna shoonla beelingeu ta tu…'

The gossamer web of words came again and again wrapping themselves around her. Butterflies tugged her belly giving her a slight feeling of nausea. It was as if she was being pulled by an invisible cord, just like those she had seen when lambs were born. It was drawing her towards the edge of her hiding spot. Lured and enticed, she knew more than anything that she had to move towards the dream like woman before her.

'Omna shoonla beelingeu ta

Omna shoonla beelingeu ta tu'

'Bell, come out dear one, I have been waiting for you. Daughter of the moon, your time is here dear one.'

The voice caressed her ears, sounding like music playing just for her. A safe voice. One she somehow knew whilst not knowing. One that settled in the cave of her heart like a loving motherly embrace.

'Omna shoonla beelingeu ta

Omna shoonla beelingeu ta tu'

Catching the words, they floated in her head, causing her to blink again.

Tremors. Beat. Pulse. Tugging.

Her head wobbled a little as she felt a warmth between her legs, a new strange sticky feeling. A cold sweat formed on her face and a dampness under her arms. There was no urge to pee, just a feeling coming from the hidden place deep within, the one the grandmothers called 'The Secret'. Rising slowly from her spot, she moved shyly towards the woman. Wincing as each tiny step felt like eggs shells cutting into the soles of her feet. She willed her legs back to life as she stumbled, following the gentle whisper which was calling her closer.

'Welcome Bell, I am Luna. I have been waiting for you. Your time is here dear one. Come! There is nothing to fear but fear itself, little woman.'

Little woman? No one had ever called her that before. Curiosity pulled at her aching heart as she overrode the fear that gripped her belly. She edged closer, watching as Luna continued weaving her invisible threads. The woman's skin shone with hues of silver and white. She had never seen anyone so beautiful, so luminous, so moonlike - La Luna herself.

'Bell, Sweet woman-child, stay. You are Bell, beloved daughter, friend, and woman becoming. Come closer.'

Luna made a final gesture in the air like a pointed star and pressing her hands into her chest, bowed to her namesake, and turned. Pearly white teeth, each one a little moon itself, beamed at her. Bell felt her tight animal body soften as she saw a welcome in the kind brown eyes that gazed upon her. Eyes that reminded her of the seals she loved to watch playing off the rocks.

'Bell, beloved, I have waited a long time to welcome you to this moment where you are 'little Bell' no more; to welcome you to the joyous and magical threshold of womanhood.'

Joyous and magical? Vaguely, she remembered being forced to sit to the side as her mother chatted with different women. She recollected listening to stories shared around tables and fires discussing the 'old-ways'. Increasingly these days, her mother repeatedly moans about 'the curse', taking herself to bed with a bottle and some pills once a month. Bell was then left to fend for herself, usually when the moon shone fully lighting the whole sky, just like tonight.

In some ways being left alone was a blessing from the common alternative which was screeching tantrums. Parts of her were afraid of this impending time, afraid of the outbursts that lay ahead if her mother was anything to go by. Yet, something deeper gnawed within her, something that yearned to believe it could be different, that there was another way. Her belly and heart told her that there was more to this than pain and suffering, that there was more to this time. There was something magical. She doubted she'd ever know what, as she listened to her mother and the other women moaning and groaning about their 'monthly curse'.

'…but I haven't started my bleed yet…' as the splutter of words left her lips more cramping gripped her belly, more stickiness formed at her 'Secret'.

Luna, smiled, nodding her head looking down at her - 'I know it is what you have been waiting for dear one, the bleed, the moon time flow, no curse, simply part of becoming a woman, one who can live in harmony with nature, one who can follow the cycles of the moon. Come bathe and see.'

The increasing discomfort of the sticky feeling between her legs made her curious to check what was going on down there. She still didn't have an urge to pee. This felt different - warm, thick, oozing. Part of her worried something was wrong with her, perhaps she too was dying? She'd watched her favourite dog die after birthing the last of her 8 pups. It had broken her heart as she'd held her gentle friend close, watching the blood flow from the place where the pups had emerged, unable to stop it. The memory hurt deeply. She didn't need to pinch herself to check she wasn't dreaming. Her tender heart and hot tears told her that this was real enough.

Her feet sank into the cool wet sand as slowly, shyly, one by one she began to remove her clothes hesitating when it came to her favourite knickers. Luna gestured at her to continue. Bell froze, fear gripped her belly tight. There in the centre of the cloth, in the gentle silvery moonlight, she saw a small patch of bright red blood. Wide eyes noticed Luna's gentle smile. Caught between fear and pure surprise, the corners of Bell's mouth raised towards the moon as she realised - yes, finally her time had come. At last, she was no longer 'little Bell'. She too, was a

'Daughter of the Moon'. She was one of those she had only dreamed about.

'Bell, your time is here.'

Bell heard herself stutter - 'Isn't this shameful and a 'curse'?'

Luna's laugh played like a harp, further narrowing the distance between them.

'No, dear one, this is a magical time, a time of becoming. You have crossed the first major threshold of what it is to become a woman.

I know you have been told how this 'works' but many have forgotten the mystery, power, and magic of this time in a woman's life. It is a gift, not a curse. It is a time for rejoicing.'

'But so many say it's full of pain. I'm frightened' Bell hated the small, scared voice that continued to come out of her mouth. This happened when she was upset and frightened. The uncomfortable gnawing feeling clawed at her heart and throat telling her she was bad and had done something wrong.

'There is nothing to fear Bell. This happens to most, but not all women. It is a part of growing up. A time of learning about becoming a woman how we bleed without dying, our power and potential. It is why I have come; to teach you. I am someone who will be in your life at times when you need me most.'

Blinking, not sure she was hearing correctly, something deep within told her the truth of Luna's words. She remembered her prayers asking for someone to love her and look after her - a mother like those she had envied in her friends, someone loving and kind. Luna's voice bought her back -

'Many moons ago here and still in some countries, you would now be married. Here we are lucky enough to rejoice in the beauty of this time, this time of maidenhood. We celebrate learning the tides and cycles of the moon and allow ourselves to deepen our connection to her sister, the earth and to listen to the wisdom of both. We begin to understand who we are, our heart and soul song. We learn the magic of what it is to be a woman through our ancestors, the grandmothers. The stories of old, spoken from mother to daughter throughout time, many now forgotten. Nature herself teaches us how to live and die each month.

You've seen how she buds and blooms only to lose all her flowers and leaves come winter. We are cyclical beings. I know you know this deep in your bones as your mother is a Magical woman too, even though she has lost her way.'

Mother. At that word she felt herself flinch, snapping out from her soft gaze and enraptured listening. She'd never known the softness of a mother - hers was a hard and painful existence. The constant feeling of being a burden to her. A busy and angry mother whose teeth and claws hung like a stone in her chest. That familiar stab of pain and loss yanked at her heart. As she struggled to contain the deep longing to know the warm embrace and guidance of a mother at this pivotal point in her life, hot tears pricked at the back of her eyes threatening to spill down her now cool cheeks. She noticed that she no longer felt like she was burning from the inside out. That burning that so often was combined with a deep desire to run far away, to hide. For once she felt calm.

'Bell, I know this is hard for you, my love. Please know I am here to help you. These are the ways of our people, our women. Much has been lost from our traditions, but I am here to teach you. As women, over time we learn we have many gifts which, if we choose, we can share with the world.'

Tired of fighting, Bell lost control of her tears. Relief came as they gushed from her sore eyes, a hot salty lava scalding her cheeks. Her heart ripped open, raw, exposed. The cracks of loss and tears of loneliness stabbed like knives creating holes in the walls she'd built around her heart. The longing to belong, the wanting to know the gentleness of a warm loving mother lay at the core.

As Luna scooped her into a soft silky warm embrace, a curtain of hair fell gently around her creating a haven of safety and comfort. She sighed – 'This is what love and safety must feel like.'

In the container of bliss, her body trembled, and fresh rivers of tears fell to meet the ocean bed below. Salty drops of pain swallowed, welcomed by the vastness where they stood soothing the pain in her heart.

Luna rocked her gently, crooning soft words into the air around her, like feathers easing her broken heart. Wrapped in the warm embrace, the lifetime of tears began to ease. Reluctantly Bell pulled away as her wet face burnt hotter and she remembered her own naked body. Searching for her clothes, the moon illuminated a stream of bright red blood trickling down her leg. Exhausted she willed the earth to open and swallow her. Not knowing where to look or what to do, the tears again burst forth like fresh rivers running free. She felt overwhelmed by the shame threatening to bury her deep into the sand or carry her away on the tide.

'There is nothing to be embarrassed about dear one. This is sacred blood. Come wash yourself in the waters of the sea.' Luna's lyrical voice like a balm to her anxious belly eased the river of tears.

Stooping to wash the blood from her leg, the water felt soft and cool. Her fingers stopped at the place other than where she peed. Her 'Secret'. That point that throbbed and ached. An entry to her body. Sometimes she liked to touch it because it felt 'nice'. Today it was sticky and heavy with blood. She looked at her red fingers. 'How can I bleed but not die nor be so very painful?' She thought to herself. Fascinated, she swished herself clean, rinsed her hands and stood up.

Luna wove a beautiful red dress around her. She handed a miniature version to Bell who suddenly became aware of the sound of an upbeat melody sung by many voices filtering through the night sky. As Bell pulled the beautiful dress over her head, a honey glow emerged from the direction of the village. The singing became louder, she could make out

a group of women approaching. Women of all ages. Each woman carried candles, flowers, bags and bundles. Each of them sang with joyous enthusiasm.

Standing beside her, Bell could feel Luna smiling. The magical woman seemed to glow brighter the more she smiled. Bell couldn't decide who was more beautiful: the moon or the woman beside her. All she knew was that her tender heart rejoiced, feeling warm, cared for. Safe. She never wanted this feeling to end.

A hundred shades of red began to circle around them. A dance of fire in physical form darted and flashed as the women moved. Each of them resembled a living flame, a mirror of the fire now burning at the centre of the circle. She turned to Luna questioning but was told - 'Trust… just watch'. She turned back to look at the faces around her. Familiar friends and their mothers joined unknown women who smiled at her as the tiny flames were cast by the candles they held. Peering around the circle, she felt her breath and body tighten as there, dressed in flowing red silk, she recognised the face of her own mother. Smiling, her mother turned towards her. Bell had never seen her look more radiant. Peering closer, she thought she caught a glimpse of something different in her eyes. A softness. A look of kindness and love. Everything she had longed for. Fresh tears fell. She wondered if she would ever stop crying! Was it a trick through a haze of tears in the moon and candlelight, or did she see a slight resemblance of Luna in her mother? Blinking, the image faded away, leaving her mother illuminated by the simple candle that she held in front of her.

The moonlit air filled with the sound of a million bees as the women continued to hum. The murmur soothed her soul, igniting her heart. She followed Luna's lead and joined in, delighting in the calming sensation flooding her body.

The women approached one by one, whispering words of wisdom

'Blessings…power…potency…blood…fetility…seership…moon…love …beauty, grace, health, vitality…' Each offered mumbled blessings into the air around her, placing flowers in her hair and bundles at her feet.

Never had she felt so seen, so welcomed, so embraced, so celebrated.

Oatcakes, lengths of cloth, flowers, pots of ointment and oils, fruits, pen and paper, ink, stones, necklaces of semi-precious stones, all lay at her feet. So many beautiful, special, and sacred things - each offering given with such love.

Her breath caught at the back of her throat and fear gripped her belly, as her mother began to approach. She prepared herself for an onslaught of words but instead, she found herself thrown off guard as the familiar gentle scent of rose reached her nose. It was a scent she so loved. The thread of a memory touched her, as she remembered an offering long ago of warmth and love from this woman. This woman, her mother, now stood in front of her as Bell shyly gazed at her beauty. The smile was returned - a long-lost dimple in her mother's cheek danced in the light offered by the flame.

'Beautiful Bell, sweet daughter. I know not what to say. It has taken for you to come to this stage in life for me to realise my errors. I call on the sisters around us here to hear me and help me to honour you as you move through this part of your life. I do not wish for you to suffer as I have. There is no need. My broken heart will mend in time. My sisters will help me heal. That has never been your job. Now it is time for you to shine, to grow wings, to learn the ways of our ancestors and to become your own medicine woman in time.

Know this, I LOVE YOU. More than life itself. It may not have always seemed this way, but it is the truth.

Daughter of mine, could you learn to forgive me?'

The words so long yearned for, hung like diamonds in the space between them. Not knowing what to do or what to believe, he looked to Luna.

Smiling with eyes full of the wisdom of all the heavens, Luna spoke 'Little woman, this is your prayer being answered. This is the medicine you have called for. The love of the mother. It is yours to take. Or not. It is time to learn your Truth. To begin to Listen. Truth and Listening are the fundamentals of knowing the ways of being a woman. It is time to begin.'

As she looked between Luna and her mother, her mother offered her a piece of pure white cloth with several simple symbols embroidered in golden thread.

She recognised the symbols which danced on the cloth like magical works of art:

Maiden. Protection. Friendship. Mother. Love.

Each tiny stitch winked at her on the beautiful fabric, shining in the gentle light of the circle. She could feel the power of each symbol - the love and care taken to create such beauty. Never had her mother given her anything so beautiful. She felt she would melt and become the ocean from the waves of grief and love that flooded her exhausted body.

'Mother I am ashamed to say it, but I have hated you and loved you equally. I don't understand what you are going through but I want my journey to be different. I am willing to try. It won't be easy'. Her voice, surprisingly, was clear and strong.

She watched as her mother's face looked sad and tears formed in her eyes.

'I understand that daughter. I can't undo the past, but I can begin to make the changes now, if you will let me?'.

Watching her, something within Bell melted, as she found herself falling into her mother's arms. Roses, silk, salty tears and humming all wrapped up in the arms of the one she had so missed. Tired of fighting she gave up to the feeling of 'home' here in her mother's embrace. Enveloped within the circle, she felt the warmth of her mother's hands as they stroked her hair and back, just as Luna had done. Each stroke, a salve, easing the pain in her broken heart. Each stroke wiping away tears and years of sadness. Each stroke bringing her back home, back to hope.

Reluctantly she peeled herself away from her mother and looked up into her eyes. Here she saw her own reflection swimming in the white pools of tears that looked down on her with love. Both
smiled. Slowly. Gently.

Without releasing her hand, her mother eased herself into the circle beside her. Nestled in between Luna and her mother, she felt again the heaviness in her pelvis. Everything felt full, throbbing warm and sticky, demanding her attention. Exhausted, yet with eyes as wide as the full moon, she waited as the last woman came towards her.

Stooped in posture with long white hair hiding her face, she recognised this woman as the Wise One. The Grandmother of the village. The one some spoke of in less than kindly tones, for most feared the strange old woman.

Witch, Old Hag, Crone - previous taunting words thrown carelessly towards the one approaching. She felt her feet beginning to itch
away. Two firm but gentle hands on the small of her back stopped her.

The grandmother approached, picking her way through the gifts, humming until she stopped just in front of her, closer than anyone. As they came nose to nose, the scent of wood smoke, wool, lavender, cinnamon, and honey reached her as the old woman lifted her head. Ocean eyes met her upturned gaze. Eyes so captivating, they twinkled like she'd stolen stars from above. The grandmother appeared almost like a young maiden herself. With love rather than shame, Bell felt her cheeks flush, as she smiled for only the second time that evening. These ancient eyes seemed to be searching for the very heartbeat of her soul. Everything else around her faded as she fell deeper into the watery eyes before her.

Her body became light as all the heaviness faded away. The evening sky closed around her as the stars burned brighter. The humming sound rose and fell, creating thermals, encouraging her to fly. Bell felt wings on her back as her body welcomed the images that swam before her eyes. Bees flitting from flower to flower, flirting with them and using their long proboscis tongues to gather the prize nectar, the golden coins of precious pollen. Salmon throwing themselves in a dance as their strong bodies fought the fast-flowing rivers on their journey home to lay eggs and once spent, would pass back into the circle of life. Swans flew high above, casting shadows of angels as their wings expanded wide. They called out below to the giant oak as they flew over it, calling her to come sit with him, to know the ways of the men. Two serpents joined together with wings and silver tongue. Image after image, sensation upon sensation. She felt she was being gifted the messages through all time fed by threads that were drawn from the earth and the stars above uniting, weaving within her.

She WAS the earth and the stars above!

The humming gained momentum creating warm thermals for them to fly. As they rose into the air all became one, they floated (the old woman and Bell) laughing. The song of the wolves running with the men joined the humming, adding a deeper call to her heart as their primal howl joined the wild crescendo of sound all around. She felt their muscular bodies, the smell of their damp fur, the sweat of the men awakening her own primal instinct to cry out with gusto. A guttural sound escaped her mouth. She had no more control. Something had her heart and soul. A knowing so deep and true she could feel it pulsing through her, wave after wave of pure bliss.

SHE WAS ALIVE. THIS WAS LIFE!

Her body felt new, her skin felt like bubbles lived on the outside. She could feel, see, and sense everything she was experiencing. She was a part of everything, and everything was a part of her. She felt she could reach her arms around the whole universe.

Gently the images began to fade as the taste of salt shifted her senses. The ache in her loins brought her back to her feet on the cool earth. She could feel the gentle heat of loving hands on her back. Without questioning she had a desire to take the hot joyous tears and rub them on her heart, on her belly and where the deep ache from her bleed felt heavy. The pain eased and softened as she did so. The grandmother nodded with an affirming smile.

'Bell, daughter of Lilith!'

Silence took its place in the night air. as the old woman's rich voice rang true and clear.

'Your destiny is clear and strong dear one. You are of the lineage of the old ways. You are one of the Granddaughters of the moon, my daughter, part of my Clan. Join us! We are the Keepers of the old ways. Will you come live in the Village house with us? Will you come to learn the lore of nature, the Alchemical ways of this sacred vessel of the Goddess you are born with? This is a rare path your soul has chosen for one so young, yet you are ready. What say you Bell, daughter of Lilith, Granddaughter of the moon? Will you join us?'

Looking around at the red robed women surrounding her, and up into the beloved faces of her mother and Luna shining down at her, something deep in her belly arose. A flame in her heart ignited, and she knew this was her path. To become a Priestess of the Moon, to honour the earth and listen to the old ways. To make them the new and current ways for all. To bring fresh life into the old ways so more people understood. To honour her body and being in this life as a sacred vessel. To come home and belong. Somewhere deep in her belly, in between her legs, in her heart, she knew something made sense.

Her voice, rich and strong spoke with a truth she'd never known before: 'Yes, Grandmother. Yes. I will join you'.

Finally, a place she could belong. Home.

Images: https://www.ancientsymbols.com/pagan_symbols.html

2 RITES OF PASSAGE CEREMONY

by Sarah-Jayne Grace

Please feel free to use this as simply or elaborately as you wish – a ceremony does not have to be complex, all a ceremony needs is a good heart and a little imagination. Some of the most powerful and beautiful ceremonies I have been involved with have been simple and very minimalistic.

Let yourself be the Creatrix of your own life and bring your leadership forward, allow yourself to be guided, listen to your belly and heart and see what they say in how you might best serve your community…and above all…BRING IN THE PLAYFUL ASPECT…ceremony doesn't have to be all serious spirit and people like to have fun. Levity, levity, levity, sprinkled with good intention and love makes life a whole lot more!

I hope you get much from reading this book and playing with this ceremony. Know that I can be contacted via my websites:

www.thewildembrace.com

In love and grace, Sarah-Jayne October 2022

'INGREDIENTS'

Group of people (number is not important)

Master/Mistress of Ceremonies (this doesn't need to be a trained person simply someone who is willing to be the one to lead)

Flowers

Candles (beeswax or soy as they are clean burning and do not create chemical vapours)

Lighter

Water and container for water

Some items to 'dress' a space beautifully

Ribbon/tape something to demote a separation of the space into 2 or more halves

Items to be given as gifts and blessings – I like to use beads and a leather thong for threading the beads upon

Feathers or something to represent 'air' element (incense can also be used)

Chair (THRONE)

Items to 'feast' and celebrate (i.e., good cake!

In this case we are speaking to menarche – this can be for a young woman or an older woman who has a desire to reclaim her essence and mark this pivotal part of her own life.

SPACE

- Create a circle for those undergoing the ceremony to gather.
- Within the circle create two halves or two smaller circles within – we are dividing the space so the person/people can move from one space to another

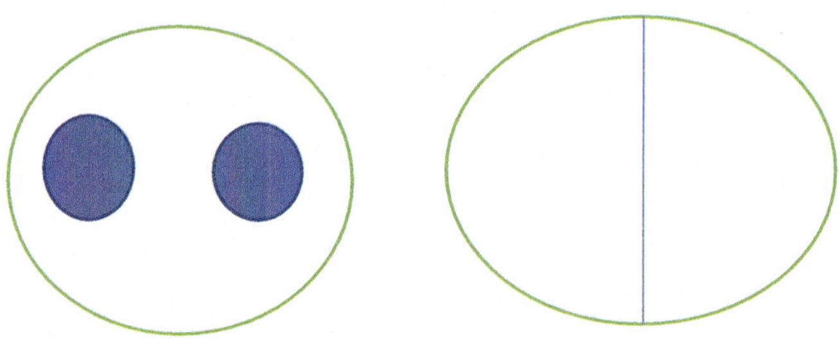

'Dress' the space.

Using flowers, fabrics, or items of nature (please use items that are naturally available and if cutting plants/trees, leave an offering of thanks to the nature spirit)

Create a throne of celebration

Create an ALTER

Items to represent the elements, may include:

Red beeswax candle

Water and container

Flowers

Feathers

PROCESS:

- Ask all attendees supporting those undergoing the ceremony to come dressed in something they feel good in: 'a celebration outfit'
- Create a circle around the denoted circle on the ground you have made
- Each person undergoing the ceremony will enter one half of the circle or one of the smaller circles (see diagrams)
- As the person enters the circle those supporting can sing a song of celebration or hum to create a warm environment
- Master/Mistress of Ceremonies to welcome everyone there in witness to the person/people undertaking the ceremony and especially the person undergoing ceremony
- Master/Mistress of Ceremonies to ask the person undergoing ceremony what they are willing to leave behind to step through into the new phase of their life
- Once the person has declared their intention for moving forward the Master/Mistress of Ceremonies will invite the person to move from one space to the next designated area

- Here the Master/Mistress of Ceremonies will ask what they are willing to invite into this new phase of their lives
- Person to declare their intention for moving forward and what they want to welcome into their lives
- Master/Mistress of Ceremonies to invite person to sit in the 'throne'
- This is an opportunity for elders in the community to offer stories if this feels right to you
- Each member of the support community to approach the throne one by one offering blessings/wishes in form of gifts and words/song.
    - This is an offering from you to them from your heart can be as short and sweet or long and elaborate as you desire. This is a beautiful process of offering love and support, perhaps guidance to the one undergoing the ROP
- Once last person has offered blessings Master/Mistress of Ceremonies to ask if there are any more words and bring everyone into a celebration song. Perhaps here everyone can move into dance so that the circle is woven anew.

- Once song has completed Master/Mistress of Ceremonies to declare ceremony closed and it is TIME TO FEAST…(and perhaps dance!)
- Create a favourite playlist of music to sing and to dance to…

3 BELLS MENARCHE AND A MODERN-DAY CEREMONY

by Rachael Crow

In the story Bell is visited by the Moon Goddess Luna who tells her that her moon time is a time of power and magic. In past times women would celebrate a young woman as they pass through this transition into womanhood with a ceremony. More and more we are realising that these celebrations and ceremonies are important, and girls are asking to have a party or gathering to honour their becoming a woman.

Shamans and Wise Elders believed ceremony was important for not only the mind and body, but also for the spirit to integrate the experience the body is going through.

A ceremony is also a way for the young person to be seen, honoured, and celebrated by their community.

Luna talked about the ancestors and the elders, in ceremony the elders would share their wisdom with the young people of the community, this was how their knowledge was passed on, through stories, songs and rituals.

In the story the women come to greet Luna with bundles, flowers, candles, and gifts, singing songs of celebration, all dressed in reds, they gathered around a fire, the oldest Grandmother stepped forward and invited her to the house of women, where the women who bled would gather- what an honour to be seen as a woman, old enough to share the women's space!

Imagine how you might like to be celebrated when it comes to your special time.

A modern Menarche celebration

This is just one example of celebrating a young woman's first blood- what we call Menarche.

Indigo asked her mum if she would help her organise a ceremony just a few weeks after her first moon time, so we gathered with a few books

and we pooled out ideas and this is what we created.
We asked the bleeding women to wear red, the moon-pause (elder) women to wear purples and blacks, and the young girls who had not yet started to wear white.

Indigo also wanted to invite her brothers, dad, uncle and grandfather- some girls only want to have women at their ceremony, but I actually think it's really important to have men at our community ceremonies, after all, men and boys need to know about the sacredness of women's moon time!

We gathered on the day in my Red Tent yurt and the women sat in circle while the men drummed outside.

We had brought flowers, red cloths, drums, and a very special cake to feast on! We smudged the space with mugwort and sage while I drummed and sang a cleansing song. Then we all introduced ourselves and we passed a small wooden bowl that held little trinkets such as crystals, a clay moon, a bottle of "moon essence", shells and threads- this is our sharing bowl- whoever holds the bowl can talk and everyone listens quietly- each women shared their story of their first moon time and any other wisdom they felt they wanted to impart to Indigo on this day.

I talked about a women's connection to the moon and how the moons cycle correlated to a woman's cycle and how deeply connected to nature and her seasons a woman's body is. How every month we go through different phases a bit like spring, summer, autumn, and winter and how powerful each of these phases are and how each of these phases hold different gifts.

We decorated a special chair for Indigo to sit on with red cloths, ribbons, and flowers and as the men came into the space- she sat on the chair, her grandmother stood at the door and asked the men if they would be respectful and honouring of the women and their space before they could enter?

She smudged them and we sat together in circle, I gave a brief her-story of red tents and how special it was to have Indigo and her family and friends together for this day.

I had prepared a large bowl of warm water with rose petals and Indigos dad washed her feet while we all sang and drummed, her friends painted her with henna and then each person brought her a gift, I had brought a red shawl that I wrapped her in and painted a moon on her forehead in red ochre (a natural paint) to symbolise her moon blood and her connection to the moon.

There were many gifts- red flowers, a moon necklace to wear when she has her moon time, soft cloth moon pads, a journal for charting her cycle, a red silk skirt, a drum, and earrings.

I asked Indigo if there was anything else she needed from us for this ceremony to feel complete- she answered chocolate cake!! Out came the cake and we feasted together before closing the ceremony with another song and final sharing, passing the bowl- everyone expressed how beautiful the day had been and how honoured they were to witness Indigo before going home.

Here are the songs we sang together.

You are beautiful

DAUGHTER OF THE MOON

You are beautiful

You are beautiful

your uniqueness fulfils a need in this world

for you are beautiful

We are beautiful

We are beautiful

Our uniqueness fulfils a need in this world

for we are beautiful

I am beautiful

I am beautiful

my uniqueness fulfils a need in this world

for I am beautiful

Born of Water

Born of Water

Cleansing,

Powerful

Healing,

Changing

We are.

How could anyone ever tell you- unknown

How could anyone ever tell you

You were anything less than beautiful

How could anyone ever tell you

You were less than whole

How could anyone fail to notice

That your loving is a miracle

How deeply you're connected to my Soul…

We are circling

We are circling

Circling together

We are singing

Singing our heart song

This is family

This is unity

This is celebration

This is sacred

I am grateful to Rachael for offering this to us and allowing me to publish it in this book.

4 THE SCIENCE OF MENARCHE

The first menstrual period and marks the completion of a girl's stepwise progression through puberty to sexual maturity,

Menarche is the first menstrual cycle, or first menstrual bleeding, in females.

It is often considered the central event of female puberty, as it signals the possibility of fertility.

Having menarche occur between the ages of 9–16 is considered normal.

Marks the time that a female can become pregnant.

The age of menarche has decreased significantly over the last 150 years.

The timing of menarche is influenced by female biology, as well as genetic and environmental factors, especially nutritional factors.

The mean age of menarche has declined over the last century.

The average age of menarche varies significantly by geographical region, race, ethnicity, and other characteristics:

Various estimates have placed it at 13.

The decline in age of menarche is observed and felt to be primarily attributed to deterioration in lifestyle factors and environmental toxic agents.

The earlier the menarche the shorter the adult stature.

There is a later age of onset in Asian populations compared to the West.

Menarche is the culmination of a series of physiological and anatomic processes of puberty.

It occurs at the attainment of a sufficient body mass, which is typically at 17% body fat.

There is disinhibition of the GnRH pulse generator in the arcuate nucleus of the hypothalamus.

Secretion of estrogen by the ovaries in response to pituitary hormones occurs.

With menarche and over an interval of about 2 to 3 years, oestrogen stimulates growth of the uterus, height growth, breast growth, widening of the pelvis, increased regional adipose tissue, and growth and vascularity of the endometrium.

No specific hormonal signal for menarche exists.

Menarche is thought to be the result of the gradual thickening of the endometrium induced by rising but fluctuating pubertal oestrogen.

The menstrual flow consists of a combination of fresh and clotted blood with endometrial tissue.

The initial flow of menarche is usually brighter than mature menstrual flow and is often scanty in amount and may be very brief, even a single instance of "spotting".

Menarche may be accompanied by abdominal cramping.

Menarche does not mean that ovulation has occurred.

In postmenarchal girls, about 80% of the cycles are anovulatory in the first year after menarche, 50% in the third and 10% in the sixth year.

The onset of regular ovulation is usually indicated by predictable and consistent intervals between menses, predictable and consistent durations of menses, and predictable and consistent patterns of menstrual flow.

Continuing ovulation typically requires a body fat content of at least 22%.

The state of potential fertility is nubility.

Some girls ovulate before the first menstruation, opposing the widely held assumption that a woman cannot become pregnant until after menarche.

Very rarely menarche may occur at an unusually early age, preceding thelarche and other signs of puberty: isolated premature menarche.

Isolated premature menarche is rarely the first manifestation of precocious puberty.

Menarche failing to occur for more than three years after thelarche, or beyond 16 years of age, delay is referred to as primary amenorrhea.

Systemic or chronic illnesses can delay menarche, such as undiagnosed and untreated celiac disease, asthma, diabetes mellitus type 1, cystic fibrosis, and inflammatory diseases.

Early age at menarche is a risk factor for the insulin resistance condition.

Factors associated with earlier menarche:

Being non-white

Having experienced pre-eclampsia in the womb

Low birthweight

Not having been breast-fed

Previous exposure to smoking

High-conflict family relationships

Increased incidence of childhood obesity.

Lack of exercise in childhood

Dire social conditions have been found to be associated with delay of maturation, an effect that may be compounded by dietary inadequacy.

Fewer than 10% of U.S. girls start to menstruate before 11 years of age, and 90% of all U.S. girls are menstruating by 13.8 years of age, with a median age of 12.4 years.

Menstruation is a cultural as well as scientific phenomenon.

Menstruation in many societies has specific rituals and cultural norms associated with it.

Used with permission from Dr S Cohen
https://standardofcare.com/menarche/

5 RESOURCES

I could write a whole book offering resources and I may well do sometime in the future!

Here I have collated a few offerings to get you started. For eco products also check your local farmers markets/health stores as they tend stock great options. Each of us has individual taste but there are so many creatives out there, those that care about our health, the earth and the keeping of the 'old ways'. You might even try making some pads yourself as part of your girls' or women's group. This is a lovely thing to do together in your journey towards your own menarche. Or even as an adult!

I have included people I know and those I don't who offer Rites of Passage as resources.

DISCLAIMER: I can take no liability for these people, they come recommended or from my own research, please speak to each person and find your perfect fit. It is your responsibility to find your way with this. If I can help I will but do your research. Ask to see their permission to work with young people. Or set up a group yourself…this is easy and empowering. Community inspires people to both gather and stand in their own power. Truly, the greatest gifts we can offer to ourselves, and our girls is to become empowered women, with heart!

PERIOD PANTS and PADS: good for the environment and your body!

Wuka Wuka.co.uk

Flux: Fluxundies.com

Thinx hiphugger organic cotton period briefs: Shethinx.com

Pantys Pantys.com

Love Luna: Sainsburys.co.uk

Modibodi: Modibodi.co.uk

Hey Girls: Heygirls.co.uk

Cocoro: Cocoro-intim.co.uk

https://www.hereweflo.co

https://ecolily.co.uk/

https://ecothes.com/blog/organic-pads

LOVELY STARTER KIT: https://www.ecoperiodpads.com/

MAKE YOUR OWN PADS: Website listing lots of resources https://sewingsociety.com/how-do-you-make-reusable-cloth-menstrual-pads-links-to-free-sewing-patterns/

RITES OF PASSAGE/BOOKS:

JOY: https://www.journeyofyoungwomen.org

I learned with Katherine and her online program has developed she also has a prolific online Facebook page https://www.facebook.com/JourneyOfYoungWomen

Rites for Girls: KIM McCabe
https://www.ritesforgirls.com/about/

Red School: fantastic teachers and resources
https://www.redschool.net/

Eartha Love https://womanbecoming.org/

6 FINAL NOTE

Finally…a note please take this story and information with what lands and leave the rest. The true path to power and embodiment is to learn to lean into life, into our hearts and into OUR TRUTH… whatever your truth, whatever your background we can make choices. We are potent beyond our wildest dreams…what you can dream can become reality…trust yourself for this is the TRUE PATH OF ENLIGHTENMENT…with love…in grace…Sarah-Jayne

7 ABOUT THE AUTHOR

Sarah-Jayne Grace is a dancer and lover of life and people. A multifaceted Teacher, Mentor and Medicine Woman she is passionate about connecting women with their full expression and beauty into the world. Years of self-flagellation and denial set her on a path of self-discovery and acceptance at a young age.

Although she has no children, she has a deep connection with her own little girl who has overcome many trials and tribulations and feels deeply about honouring and supporting our young people – our future generation!

Sarah-Jayne lives and dances in the UK, works as a Therapeutic Coach online, runs Women's groups and dances. This is her first short story that was birthed from a 2-year Creative Writing Program. Sarah-Jayne has been published in various magazines and Elephant Journal. You can find Sarah-Jayne either dancing in the wilds or in a kitchen rustling up some delights for the soul.

Website here: www.thewildembrace.com

If you would like to work with me, please get in touch

sarah@thewildembrace.com

Gwen Pawson is an inspiring 13-year-old an aspiring writer and artist Gwen has a dream of writing and travelling the world whilst lighting the way with her fiery spirit and fire poi. Gwen lives in the wilds of Devon with her family and dog Ru.

Rachael Crow: Teacher: Mentor: Medicine Woman is particularly passionate about working with women at their transitions - Menarche (first blood), Mother/ birthing yourself as a mother, Honouring hysterectomy, infertility, peri menopause and menopause.

I love bringing people to the heartbeat of our Earth Mother, to quieten ourselves and deeply listen to her messages, through our wombs, drum journeys, nature connection....

We can all pause, breathe, drop our roots down and connect to the earth any time and listen to her wisdom. I am Earth Keeper, I am the earth, I hold the earth at my center and consider her in all my actions.

https://www.rachaelcrow.co.uk/

8 FOR YOUR OWN NOTES/SONGS/REFERENCES

SONG IDEAS

CONTACTS

RESOURCES

DOODLES

PLANNING FOR CEREMONY

DREAMS

DREAMS

IDEAS

DAUGHTER OF THE MOON

SONGS

DAUGHTER OF THE MOON

Printed in Great Britain
by Amazon

87461122R00047